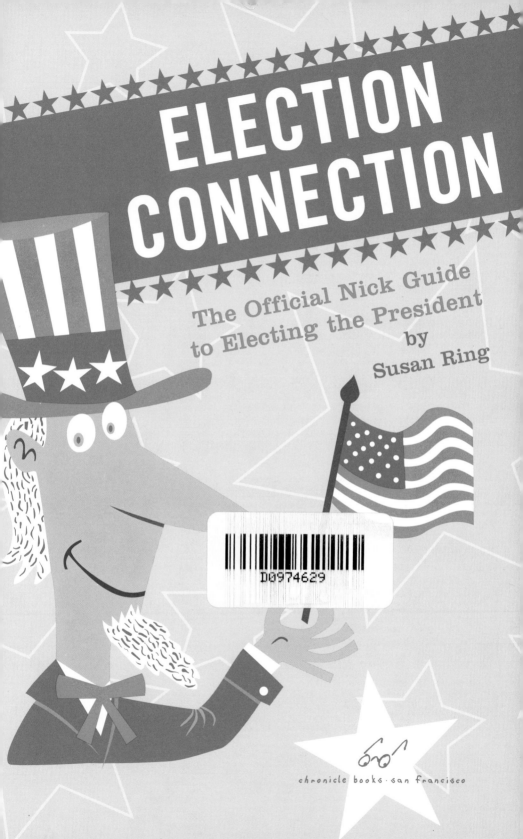

ELECTION CONNECTION

The Official Nick Guide
to Electing the President
by
Susan Ring

chronicle books · san francisco

Nickelodeon, Rugrats, Nickelodeon Rocket Power, The Wild Thornberrys, SpongeBob SquarePants,
Hey Arnold, The Adventures of Jimmy Neutron: Boy Genius, Fairly OddParents, and all related titles,
logos, and characters are trademarks of Viacom International Inc. Rugrats, Nickelodeon Rocket
Power, and The Wild Thornberrys created by Klasky Csupo, Inc. SpongeBob SquarePants created by
Stephen Hillenburg. Hey Arnold created by Craig Barlett. Fairly OddParents created by Butch
Hartman.

Book design by Kristen M. Nobles.
Typeset in Clarendon and Trade Gothic.
Illustrations on pages 1, 6, 10, 11, 12–13, 25, 28, 29, 30, 31, 35, 38, 40, 42–43, 50, 51, 60–61, 63, 64, 66, 70, 74
by David Sheldon.
Cover photographs by Danni Steele.
Manufactured in China.

Library of Congress Cataloging-in-Publication Data
Election connection : the official nick guide to electing the president.
        p. cm.
Summary: Addresses issues surrounding a Presidential election including
media, ballot issues, liberal and conservative viewpoints, election
budgets, travel, and campaigning.
        ISBN 0-8118-4175-8
1. Presidents—United States—Election—Juvenile literature.
2. Elections—United States—Juvenile literature. 3. Voting—United
States—Juvenile literature. 4. Political campaigns—United
States—Juvenile literature. [1. Presidents—Election. 2. Elections.
3. Voting. 4. Politics, Practical.] I. Nickelodeon (Firm)
JK528.E43 2004
324.973'0931—dc22

                    2003015904

Distributed in Canada by Raincoast Books
9050 Shaughnessy Street, Vancouver, British Columbia V6P 6E5

10 9 8 7 6 5 4 3 2 1

Chronicle Books LLC
85 Second Street, San Francisco, California 94105

www.chroniclekids.com
www.nick.com

CONTENTS

CONTENTS (continued)

CHAPTER 1

VOTING
People Do It
Every Day

VOTE, VOTE, AND VOTE AGAIN!

Even though you haven't voted in a presidential election yet, chances are you have voted. Maybe you have voted to elect members of your school's student council. Maybe you voted in Nickelodeon's Kid's Choice Awards. When you tell your parents whether you'd like hamburgers or spaghetti for dinner, your answer is a vote!

WHAT IS A DEMOCRACY?

The word *democracy* describes a government by the people, in which citizens exercise their power by voting. In our democracy, we have rights that include being able to express our opinions, receive a free education, and practice any religion that we choose. U.S. citizens won and protected these rights through voting.

Having the right to vote is part of living in a democracy. And exercising that right is a way for citizens to take responsibility for—and take part in—their government.

THE LAST THING I VOTED FOR WAS_____

_____

_____

THE RESULTS_____

_____

_____

I WOULD / WOULD NOT VOTE THE SAME WAY AGAIN

POWER TO THE PEOPLE!

The word *democracy* comes from two Greek words:

'DEMOS" (PEOPLE) -

"KRATOS" (POWER)
= DEMOCRACY

The United States is much too large for every single person to personally take part in running the government. Can you imagine going to a meeting with everyone in town... and every other town in the whole country? Where would it be held? There is no place big enough. Besides, nobody would stay awake long enough to listen to all the opinions! But fear not! You can still be heard.

The United States has what is called a *representative democracy*. That means we choose people to represent our views in the government. We vote, and the elected people do all the work!

THE CONSTITUTION AND THE THREE BRANCHES OF GOVERNMENT

Our Constitution was written more than 200 years ago, when the United States of America was a brand-new nation. The founders of the country wanted to create a free country where the government served the people. And so they wrote the Constitution. The Constitution set down the laws and guiding principles for the government and the people of the new country.

When the 13 colonies were part of England, they were ruled by one person: the king of England. The founders of the United States wanted to create a system that made sure that no one person or part of the government had too much power. So they designed a system of "checks and balances." In this system, the power is divided among three branches of government.

Of the 39 delegates who signed the Constitution, 2 later were elected president of the United States. They were George Washington and James Madison.

We the People

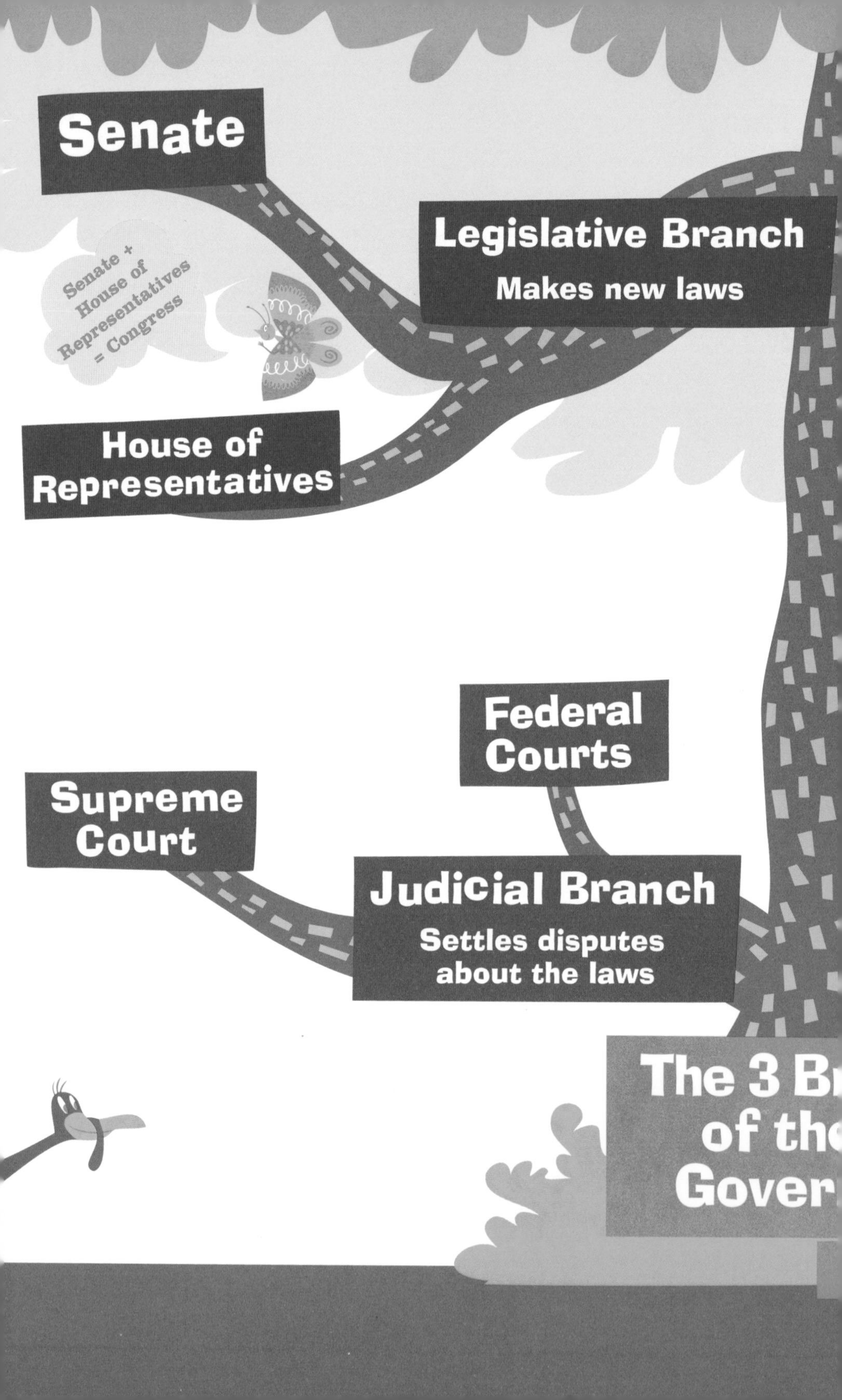

Senate

Legislative Branch

Makes new laws

Senate +
House of
Representatives
= Congress

**House of
Representatives**

**Federal
Courts**

**Supreme
Court**

Judicial Branch

**Settles disputes
about the laws**

The 3 Br
of th
Gover

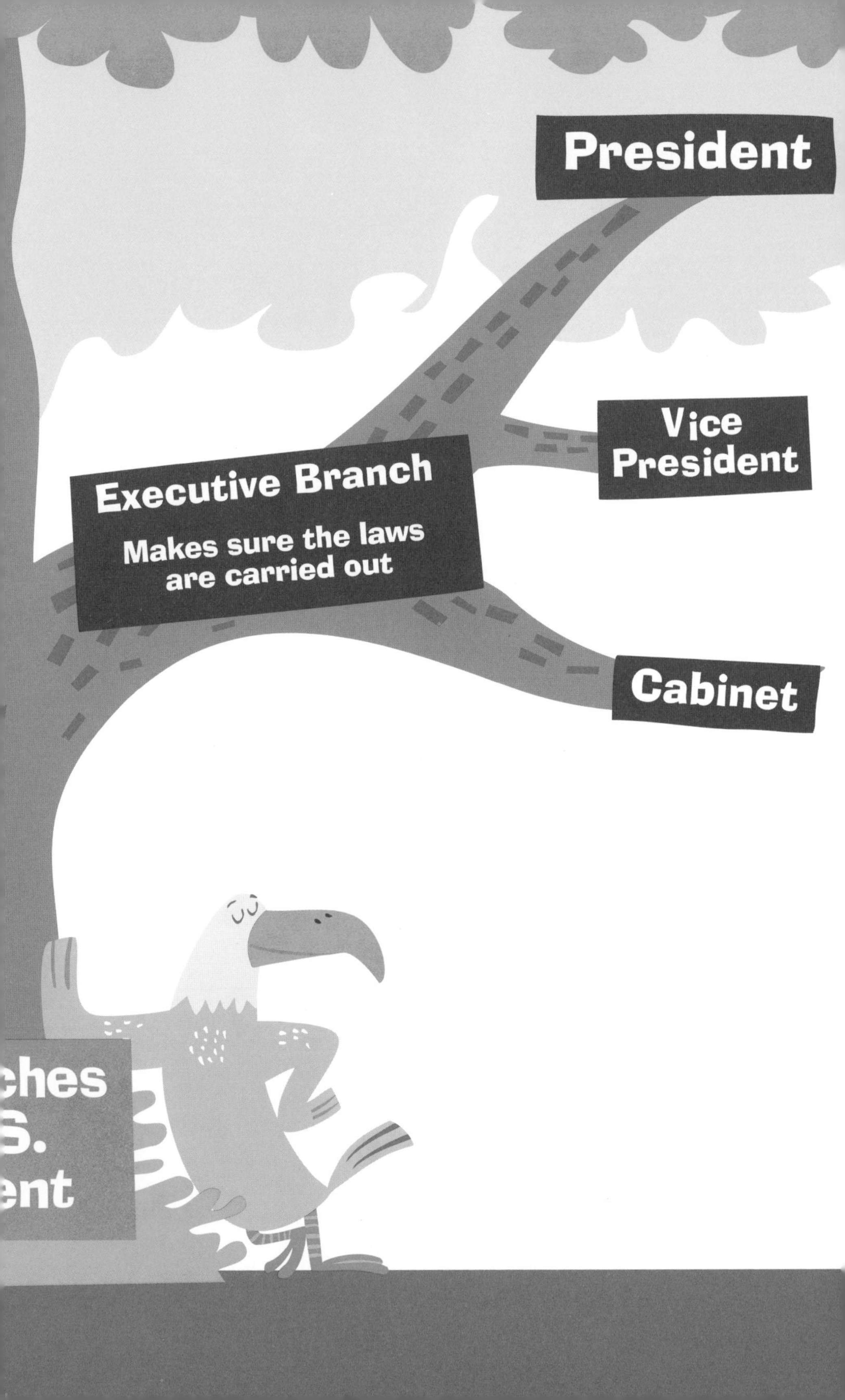

President

Vice President

Executive Branch

Makes sure the laws
are carried out

Cabinet

ches
S.
ent

DO YOU KNOW THE RULES OF VOTING?

You can vote if...
(Circle "Y" for yes or "N" for no)

You have red hair	Y	N
You are not a U.S. citizen	Y	N
You are in jail	Y	N
You have been in jail before but are now out	Y	N
You are a cartoon character	Y	N
You don't speak English	Y	N
You can't read	Y	N
You can read	Y	N
You see double	Y	N
You are not registered to vote	Y	N
You are out of town on Election Day	Y	N

Turn the page for the answers.

THE RULES

Y	Even if you have no hair you can vote.
N	Sorry, only U.S. citizens can vote.
N	In jail? Forget it.
Y	Now you're out of jail? Okay to vote.
N	Bad news for the residents of Bikini Bottom. Cartoon characters *cannot* vote.
Y	Even if you speak Martian, you can vote.
Y	Make sure you can read whom you're voting for!
Y	If you cn rd ths, thn you cn vte.
YY	You can vote if you see double. But you can't vote twice!
Y+N	You must register to vote in every state except one. See page 18.
Y	If you are out of town, you can send in an absentee ballot. See next chapter.

Each state makes its own rules for elections. All states agree that to vote, you must be 18 years old or older. You must also be a U.S. citizen. People in prison may not vote, although they may regain their voting rights after being released. Congress can change a state's voter requirements if it thinks that the state has broken any constitutional rules. That is an example of checks and balances.

THE RIGHT TO VOTE

Today, any U.S. citizen 18 years or older can vote, but it was not always that way. When the United States was a young nation, only white male landowners could vote. The rules for voting slowly changed, but not without great struggles.

In 1870, the government passed the 15th Amendment to the Constitution. (An amendment is a change or addition.) This amendment gave all men the right to vote. *(Notice, the 15th Amendment said men...not women. That would come later—after more struggles.)* The 15th Amendment said it didn't matter what someone's race was. And it said it didn't matter if you had been a slave.

But some people did not agree with the 15th Amendment. They felt that former slaves and men who did not own land should not have the right to vote. So some states forced voters to take difficult reading tests or pay high poll taxes in order to vote. This discouraged poor men, especially those who had been slaves, from voting.

This continued in some states into the 1960s, almost 100 years after the 15th Amendment was passed! But in 1964, the 24th Amendment was passed. It made poll taxes illegal. And in 1965, the Voting Rights Act was passed. It made it illegal to force voters to take literacy tests.

REGISTERING TO VOTE

Before an election, you must register to vote. Registering to vote means that you are officially "signing up" to vote. It is very easy to register to vote. Depending on the state, you can register at places like the post office, the bank, or even by mail.

VOTING RIGHTS FOR WOMEN

The 15th Amendment did not grant women the right to vote. Women fought very hard for that. The fight was called Women's Suffrage, and it lasted for decades! In 1848, Elizabeth Cady Stanton and Lucretia Mott organized the first convention for women's rights. It was held in Seneca Falls, New York. In 1869, two organizations were formed to work to give women the right to vote: the American Woman Suffrage Association and the National Woman Suffrage Association. Cady Stanton and Susan B. Anthony were the leaders of the National Woman Suffrage Association.

WHICH ONE OF THESE IS A REAL COIN?

If you guessed the third one, you are right. It is the Susan B. Anthony dollar coin. Susan B. Anthony was the first woman to appear on American currency.

Here comes another amendment! In 1878, a constitutional amendment for women's suffrage was brought before Congress. It did not pass. But that didn't stop people from trying. It was presented to every session of Congress for four decades—that's 40 years! By 1919, the amendment had passed in the House of Representatives and in the Senate. It then had to be voted on by each state. In 1920, enough states approved it, and it became the 19th Amendment. It says that no one can be denied the right to vote because of his or her sex.

CHANGING THE VOTING AGE

Until the 1960s, citizens had to be at least 21 years old to vote. But in the 1960s, the United States got involved in the Vietnam War. At the age of 18, men and women could serve in the military. Many Americans believed that if a citizen could fight for the country, he or she should have the right to vote, too. The 26th Amendment was passed in 1971. It changed the legal voting age to 18.

Today, all American citizens 18 or older can vote. All of this work must have been for an important reason! Would so many people have spent so many years fighting for the right to vote if each person's vote didn't count? NO. They didn't say, "Why bother? My vote doesn't count anyway." They said, **"I WANT TO VOTE! I WANT TO HAVE A VOICE IN HOW MY COUNTRY IS RUN!"**

OLD ENOUGH TO VOTE, NOT OLD ENOUGH TO RUN

Would you like to run for president? You might have to wait a couple of years! Even though people can vote when they are 18 years old, the Constitution says that anyone who runs for president of the United States must be 35 or older. Candidates must also have been born U.S. citizens.

WHAT DID THEY DO BEFORE THEY BECAME PRESIDENT?

Some presidents were generals. Others were lawyers or congressmen. Do you know what these presidents did before they were elected to the highest office in the land? Draw a line from each president to his former jobs.

1. Jimmy Carter

2. Andrew Jackson

3. Harry Truman

4. Ronald Reagan

5. Abraham Lincoln

6. George Washington

7. James A. Garfield

a. Actor / Governor of California

b. Peanut farmer / Governor of Georgia

c. Tailor / Governor of Tennessee

d. Clothing store owner / Senator from Missouri

e. Surveyor, farmer and businessman / Leader of the Continental Army

f. Canal boat driver, professor of classics / Senator from Ohio

g. Lawyer, farmer, rail splitter and shopkeeper / Senator from Illinois

CHAPTER 3
WAYS TO VOTE
What's Really Behind That Curtain

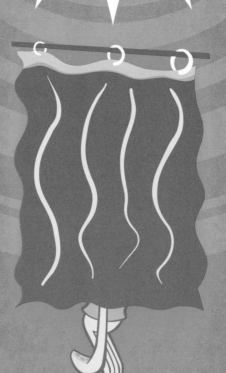

There are many ways to cast a vote. For example, your teacher might ask everyone in the class to vote on whether they want a test. He might have students who want to vote yes raise their hands. Then he would count the number of raised hands. Anyone crazy enough to vote yes for a test just might get a bunch of angry looks from classmates. So it could be a wiser idea to vote by writing "yes" or "no" in secret.

People who participate in traditional-style town meetings in New England still vote by a show of hands. But mostly, when we vote, we use voting systems that are a little more private, so there is no need to worry about what other people will think of your vote.

POLLING PLACES

A polling place is where people go to vote, such as a school or firehouse. A voter signs in, then a volunteer checks the voter's name against the voter registration list. Then the voter might be directed to a voting booth or be asked to use a paper ballot, sometimes called a punch card.

WHAT ARE BALLOTS?

Whether voting by machine or by paper punch cards, we use ballots to cast our votes. In colonial times, political parties passed out lengthy "tickets" for each party. Voters were asked to vote a "straight party ticket." That means they voted only for candidates belonging to one party. That's why we still call a group of candidates from the same party "a ticket." But today we have a single ballot that lists all candidates from all political parties.

VOTING MACHINES

You might be familiar with the voting machine—that little booth with a curtain around it. But do you know what's inside that mysterious little booth? Usually there is a panel that lists the candidates. Beside each candidate's name is a lever or a button. You pull a lever

(or press a button) for each candidate you wish to vote for. When you pull the curtain open to exit the booth, the levers go back the way they were. That way each person's votes are kept secret.

PUNCH CARDS

Another way to vote is by punch-card ballot. Voters are given a punch card that lists the candidates. Next to each candidate's name is a hole that can be punched out. The voter punches holes in the card to indicate his or her votes.

AHA!

The word *ballot* comes from the Italian word *ballotta*. *Ballotta* were little colored balls used to cast votes in the 13th century.

THE BUTTERFLY CREATES TROUBLE

In the 2000 presidential election, a punch card called the "butterfly" ballot caused a lot of confusion in Florida. Some of the ballots were two pages long, and voters accidentally selected two candidates. These ballots were thrown out, because the choice of candidate wasn't clear. Also, some of the holes punched in the cards didn't go all the way through. The voting machines could not read these partially punched ballots.

The election was a close race between Vice President Al Gore and candidate George W. Bush. Votes had to be recounted in several Florida counties. It was all finally settled by the U.S. Supreme Court—a first in American history.

ELECTRONIC VOTING

There are several types of electronic voting methods. One is called Direct Recording Electronic (DRE). Inside the DRE voting machine is a computer.

The candidates are listed on the computer screen, and you vote by touching the screen.

ABSENTEE BALLOTS

Away during an election? No problem. You can still vote by using an absentee ballot. This is a ballot that you mail to the government so that your vote can be counted even if you can't get to the voting polls on Election Day. Often, people in the military and college students vote this way.

EXIT POLLS

"Who did you vote for?" That's an exit poll. During elections, pollsters and members of the press try to find out whom people are voting for. They wait outside polling places and ask, "Who got your vote?" By keeping track of the answers, they try to predict who will win the election.

OOPS!

Pollsters and reporters aren't always right in their election predictions. In 1948, the *Chicago Tribune* printed the headline "Dewey Defeats Truman" on the front page of the paper before all the votes were counted. The pollsters had quit too early in the day—it was Harry Truman who won the election, not Thomas Dewey!

CHAPTER 4

POLITICAL PARTIES

Am I Invited?

WHAT IS A POLITICAL PARTY?

A political party is an organized group of people with similar political goals and viewpoints. Members of a political party work together to elect government representatives from their party. They choose candidates who have the same beliefs and goals that they do.

The members of a political party help their candidates run for office. This includes organizing the campaign and raising money. Volunteering for a political party gives the average citizen a way to get more involved in politics.

WHY DO WE NEED POLITICAL PARTIES?

Different groups of people have different views. We all like to have choices. Having more than one political party spices things up—it encourages debate about different issues. What do you think it would be like if there were only one political party in the United States?

BIG PARTIES AND THEIR HISTORIES

The United States currently has two main political parties—the Democrats and the Republicans. There are also smaller political parties in the United States, known as *third parties*. These parties are created for several reasons. Sometimes people want to support a particular candidate, so a party forms around the candidate. In 1912, the Progressive, or Bull Moose, Party was formed in order to nominate Theodore Roosevelt for a third term as president. He didn't win, but he did come in second.

RETROVILLE NEWS

POLITICAL RALLY IN RETROVILLE

DNA EXPANDS TO NEW OFFICES

Other times, people form political parties based on a particular issue. For example, the Green Party focuses on environmental issues. Third parties and independent candidates give voters more choices. They also promote new ideas. They are just as interested in bringing attention to the issues they believe are important as they are in winning the election.

PARTY SYMBOLS: THE ELEPHANT AND THE DONKEY

In 1874, a political cartoon showed an elephant running away from a donkey, the Democratic symbol. Lettering on the elephant said "Republican Vote." Over time these animals became the symbols of the two parties. The Democrats think the elephant is stupid, but the Republicans think it is strong and intelligent. On the other hand, the Democrats think their donkey is smart and loveable while the Republicans think it is stubborn and silly. What do you think?

IF YOU WERE TO FORM A POLITICAL PARTY, WHAT WOULD IT STAND FOR? _____

_____

_____

_____

WHAT WOULD YOU CALL IT?

_____

_____

DESIGN A SYMBOL THAT YOU WOULD USE TO REPRESENT YOUR OWN POLITICAL PARTY.

CHAPTER 5

CAMPAIGNS

Pick Me!
Pick Me!

CONVENTIONS: PARTIES FOR THE PARTIES

The summer before every presidential election, the major political parties hold conventions. A political convention seems more like a party than a political meeting! It is filled with balloons, confetti, celebrities, noise, and lots of red, white, and blue signs. However, some very important things happen at political conventions. The convention is where delegates choose the presidential nominee. Usually, the nominee was decided months before. The convention is where the nomination is officially announced and approved. After the presidential nominee is officially selected, he or she names a running mate for vice president.

SIGNS, BANNERS, AND BUTTONS

If you watch a political convention on television, you may notice people holding signs showing their candidate's name. You'll probably see people wearing buttons, hats, and T-shirts supporting their candidate, too. People often collect these souvenirs. Looking through a collection of political memorabilia will give you a little history about the campaigns of the past.

PLATFORMS: NOT JUST TO STAND ON

Another important thing that happens at a political convention is the approval of the party's platform. A platform describes what the party stands for. The presidential nominees try to communicate the messages of their platforms to the public during their campaigns.

THE CAMPAIGN TRAIL: ON THE ROAD AGAIN

In 1948, President Harry S Truman traveled by train across the United States to campaign for reelection. He traveled more than 31,000 miles and made over 350 speeches on his "whistle-stop tour"! His down-to-earth style appealed to many voters.

When it comes to running for president, there are actually two political elections. The first is called the *primary election.*

PRIMARY ELECTIONS

In the primary election each political party elects its nominee (candidate). These elections take place over several months. The winning candidates then move on to represent their parties in the *general election.*

GENERAL ELECTIONS

In the general election the candidates try to get votes from everyone, not just from members of their own political party. The candidate who wins the general election becomes the next president.

During both campaigns, candidates spend months on the road. They travel from state to state, trying to reach as many people as possible. Often, they will show up at rallies and meetings of different organizations. Candidates strive for the personal touch—shaking hands, kissing babies, and getting up close to talk to, and meet, average citizens. Often, the candidates' families travel with them on the campaign trail. Their husbands or wives and children proudly stand by their side. Why do you think they do this?

CLINTON BY CAMERA

In 1992, when William Jefferson Clinton ran for president, he went on late-night TV shows to reach voters. He also appeared on *Nick News* to share and discuss his views.

VOTE FOR ME!!

Create a sample button, sign, or bumper sticker with your slogan on it.

IF YOU WERE RUNNING FOR POLITICAL OFFICE, WHAT WOULD YOUR SLOGAN BE?

_____

_____

_____

_____

DEFINE YOUR PLATFORM.

_____

_____

_____

_____

_____

_____

_____

CHAPTER 6

THE MEDIA
The Good, the Bad, and the Ugly

HOW WILL YOU EVER DECIDE ON A CANDIDATE?

You might think it's easy to pick a candidate. You'll just watch the commercials and read the ads. They tell the truth about who the best candidates are.

NOT!

Candidates spend a lot of money on advertising. But remember: The goal of these ads is to get votes.

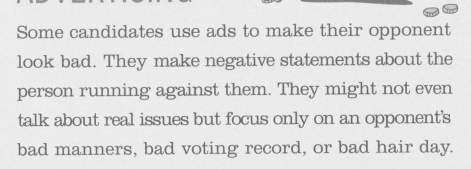

NEGATIVE ADVERTISING

Some candidates use ads to make their opponent look bad. They make negative statements about the person running against them. They might not even talk about real issues but focus only on an opponent's bad manners, bad voting record, or bad hair day.

It may be nasty, but is it against the rules? Not always.

What do you think of the following ad?

"Joan Sloan voted against a law that protected the environment. She obviously is not a fighter for cleaner water and air. Remember that— as you go coughing and hacking into the voting booth."

Joan Sloan would be a lousy choice, don't you think? But the ad didn't mention that Joan voted against the law because she felt the law wasn't tough enough. That's a story you won't hear unless you do some further digging on your own.

So you see, negative advertising may actually help you make an informed decision. It can give you ideas for questions to ask and things to think about. Many people think that negative advertising is something new. But the truth is, negative campaigning has been around for a long time. Candidates used it long before television was invented.

THE IMPACT OF TELEVISION

Before people had televisions, candidates used their party members to spread the word about their platforms and their campaigns. Television gave candidates a way to reach voters directly. Now, it isn't always a candidate's voting record, or point of view, that wins votes. Often, the reason a candidate gets votes—or doesn't—is how he or she looks on camera. Maybe a candidate was wearing a really awesome jacket. Would that make you think that she would do a good job? Whether we like it or not, television can make us judge a person based on what they look like.

Candidates often hire consultants—people who tell them what to wear and how to present them-selves to the public. They think this will make them more popular and win them more votes.

Often, politicians, businesspeople, and community leaders will speak on behalf of a candidate. The hope is that by having someone important say good things about a candidate, it will influence voters to choose him or her. Let's say that your favorite television star speaks in favor of a particular candidate. You might say, "If *he* likes her, I like her!" Who would influence you to vote for someone?

POLITICAL CARTOONS: THAT'S NOT FUNNY!

Political cartoons are featured in newspapers, magazines, and on web sites all over the world. With a few words and simple, clever images, political cartoonists can say a lot. Political cartoons often make fun of the issues or of a candidate. They can simplify complicated issues. They are not supposed to be just funny. They are meant to make you think.

Did you know that Dr. Seuss began his career as a political cartoonist? Before he became a children's book author, he created political cartoons for a daily New York newspaper called *PM*.

Benjamin Franklin created one of the earliest political cartoons in 1754. The cartoon showed a snake cut up into pieces. Each piece was labeled with a colony's name. The caption said, "JOIN, or DIE." Franklin's message was that the colonies would be strong if they joined together as one, but if they separated, like the snake, they would not survive.

Political cartoonists use their cartoons to express their own opinions on issues, just like Franklin did.

HOW TO BE AN INFORMED VIEWER

🌟 Read between the lines of ads to see what they imply, rather than what they actually say. Ask yourself, "Was that out of line?"

🌟 Read the news. But remember: News organizations may have their own points of view. They can present information in a way that includes some facts and leaves out others.

Dear Sir,,
Is it true that you voted for a new law that will make home-work illegal?

🌟 Don't be distracted by how the candidates look. What really counts is what they believe in and what they say they will do.

🌟 Go straight to the candidates! Write letters or e-mails to ask about issues directly.

MY HEAD IS SPINNING

Here are two versions of the same speech. It is up to you to fill in the blanks. One should have a positive spin—the other a

Positive Spin

I am here to tell you that I am the best candidate. I have a _ _ _ _ _ _ _ _ record, which shows that I am _ _ _ _ _ _ _ _ . But, first, let me tell you about my opponent. My opponent is not _ _ _ _ _ _ _ _ . She is _ _ _ _ _ _ _ _ . Some people say that she is _ _ _ _ _ _ _ _ . Now, that is something to pay attention to. As for me, the main point is that you should all vote for me because I am _ _ _ _ _ _ _ _ .

funny
cool
a dork
a bad person
honest
a bad dresser
inexperienced

negative spin. Try it! Use the words/phrases provided or make up your own. You'll see how with just a few words the entire meaning of something can change.

Negative Spin

I am here to tell you that I am the best candidate.

I have a _____ record, which shows that I am

_____. But, first, let me tell you about

my opponent. My opponent is not _____.

He is _____. Some people say that he is

_____. Now, that is something to pay

attention to. As for me, the main point is that you

should all vote for me because I am _____.

fair
unfair
the best person for the job
clueless
smart
hardworking
dishonest

During campaigns, candidates often *debate* each other. That means that they stand up in front of people—sometimes on TV—and take turns giving their opinions. Debates are like organized and ever-so-polite arguments. The candidates use debates to try to convince voters to agree with their view of the issues. Voters use debates to learn more about the candidates.

Usually in a debate, one person—not a candidate—acts like a referee. This is the moderator. The moderator asks questions and sets time limits for the candidates' answers. The candidates take turns answering the questions asked by the moderator. They don't usually know these questions ahead of time. But they can guess what the questions will be and prepare for them, just like you might study for a test at school.

When you listen to a debate, you might notice that the candidates don't always answer the question asked. It's the moderator's job to try to keep them on track. Candidates are usually given the chance to make statements at the start and end of the debate. That's when they can give their opinions on anything they want to.

Debates are nothing new. A dramatic series of debates took place in 1858 between Stephen Douglas and Abraham Lincoln. The candidates were both running in Illinois for a seat in the U.S. Senate. Douglas was an excellent speaker. Lincoln at that time wasn't very well known. But he was funny and smart, so he made a good impression. There was no TV or radio in 1858, but thousands of people went to hear the debates in person. And through word of mouth, as well

Squidward here would have you believe that all I do is eat and sleep. He speaks not the truth. I also watch television.

as through the newspapers, Lincoln gained fame throughout the country. He didn't win the Senate seat, but two years later he was elected president.

Douglas and Lincoln did not have to face the cameras and bright lights of a debate on television. But in 1960, Richard Nixon and John F. Kennedy did. Theirs was the first presidential debate to be broadcast on national television. Millions of people tuned in. Kennedy looked good on TV. He looked young and relaxed. Nixon looked tired and nervous. Sweat showed on his face. "Who cares?" you might say. "It's what they say that's important. Not how they look."

Well, who won that debate? Those who heard it on the radio thought Nixon had won. Those who saw the two on television believed that Kennedy won! What does that tell you?

In the end, John F. Kennedy won the race for president.

CHAPTER 8

THE ELECTORAL COLLEGE

Does Anyone Ever Graduate from There?

The electoral college isn't a school. It's the group of people who actually vote for president. What is *that* all about? Well, even though we vote for our president and vice president every four years, we don't directly elect them. Really we are voting for groups of people called electors, who vote for us.

HUH? How did this come about?

Our founding fathers thought about having Congress elect the president. But no: Always careful about checks and balances, they worried that this would give Congress too much power. They also considered the idea of having citizens elect the president directly. Whomever got the most votes would be president. No again: They were afraid that people would only vote for the candidates within their state or region. They worried that no candidate would get a majority of votes. Or that only candidates from states with a lot of people would be able to win.

In the end, the founding fathers decided that the president would be elected by representatives from each state. These people would be called electors. Each state would have a number of electors equal to the number of its members in Congress.

In most states, the candidate who wins the most votes wins all the electoral votes from that state. So even if one candidate got 49% (while the other got 51%) he or she would win *no* electoral votes.

After the general election, on the first Monday after the second Wednesday in December, the electors meet in their state capitols to officially vote for the president and vice president. The results of the election are known well before the electors vote. The process is mostly a formality. The votes are then certified and sent to the president of the Senate, who unseals and counts the votes in front of Congress. The candidate with the most electoral votes becomes the next president of the United States.

In the election of 1800, Thomas Jefferson ran for president against John Quincy Adams. At that time, electors cast two votes but didn't indicate which vote was for president and which was for vice president.

So Thomas Jefferson and Aaron Burr—Jefferson's running mate for vice president—each received the same number of votes. The election was a tie between the two running mates! It was up to the House of Representatives to decide the winner. After 36 rounds of voting, on February 7, the House ultimately confirmed Thomas Jefferson as president and Aaron Burr as vice president. In order to avoid this situation in the future, the 12th Amendment was passed. Electors now cast two separate votes: one for president, and one for vice president.

Electors are expected to vote for the candidate whom they have pledged to support. But legally, they don't have to. There have been at least 8 times in the history of presidential elections when electors did not. This has never changed the outcome of an election but has come pretty close! In 1968 an elector from North Carolina who was to vote for Nixon, instead voted for independent candidate, George Wallace. As a result Wallace gained North Carolina's 46 electoral votes. It almost prevented Nixon, the Republican candidate, from getting the number he needed to win the election.

Alaska
3

Washington
11

Montana
3

Idaho
4

Oregon
7

Wyoming
3

Utah
5

Colorado
8

Nevada
4

Arizona
8

California
54

New
Mexico
5

Hawaii
4

ELECTORAL VOTES

This map shows the number of electoral votes in each state. How many does your state have? Which states do you think candidates will most want to win?

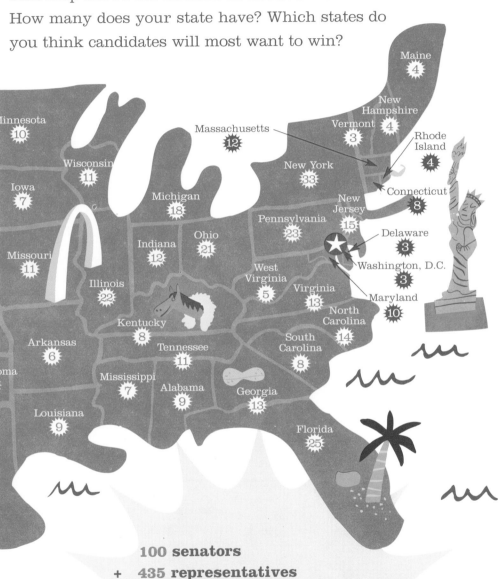

Maine 4
New Hampshire 4
Vermont 3
Rhode Island 4
Connecticut 8
New York 33
New Jersey 15
Delaware 3
Washington, D.C. 3
Maryland 10
Massachusetts 12
Minnesota 10
Wisconsin 11
Iowa 7
Michigan 18
Pennsylvania 23
Ohio 21
Indiana 12
Missouri 11
Illinois 22
West Virginia 5
Virginia 13
North Carolina 14
Kentucky 8
Arkansas 6
Tennessee 11
South Carolina 8
Mississippi 7
Alabama 9
Georgia 13
Louisiana 9
Florida 25

100 **senators**
+ 435 **representatives**
+ 3 **electors for Washington, D.C.**

---

538 **total number of electors**
270 **electoral votes are needed to win the presidency**

So, when exactly do people vote? Is there any rhyme or reason to it? It can be complicated, but here goes:

General elections take place on Election Day. We elect members of the House of Representatives every two years, senators every six years, and the president and vice president every four years.

Election Day is the first Tuesday after the first Monday in November. Sound strange? Well, there is some logic behind this choice.

Throughout most of its history, the United States was a farming society. In early November, the harvest was over and the worst winter weather hadn't arrived yet. So early November was a good time for farmers to travel to the polls to vote. But the founding fathers didn't want Election Day to fall on the first day of November for two reasons. First, it is a religious holiday—All Saints' Day. Second, the first day of the month was once a busy day for merchants. They used that day to do their accounting.

Also, it was decided that Election Day shouldn't be on a Monday because many people would have to travel far to get to polling places. Since Sundays were devoted to religious worship, Monday would have to be the travel day. So it was decided that Election Day would be the first Tuesday following the first Monday in November.

Whew!

WHAT A DAY!

On Election Day, campaign signs line streets. Voters hurry to the polls. Radio stations, television stations, and newspapers buzz with activity. Excitement is in the air. This is especially true if it is a presidential election year.

When polling places close on the East Coast, the first actual results are reported. News programs show a map of the United States, and as the final vote counts come in, the map is shaded to show the winner in each state. The news reports continue until all the polls have closed. Sometimes an election is a landslide—that means that one candidate has won by a large number of votes. Other races are extremely close, and a winner cannot be determined until late that night or even the next day!

Sometimes networks predict election results too soon. This happened in the 2000 presidential election. Television stations first reported that Vice President Al Gore had won the state of Florida. Florida is an important swing state. That means it is not definitely Democratic or Republican. It could "swing" either way. However, all the votes weren't in. Then television stations started saying that actually Bush had won the election. When it turned out that the race was too close to call, the networks had to admit they were wrong *again!* The entire presidential election was up in the air because of one state. After many arguments, discussions, and recounts, George W. Bush won Florida's 25 electoral votes...and the presidential election.

The numbers are in...

You can see it is not a good idea to count on reported election results before all of the polls have closed and all the votes have been counted. Citizens who haven't voted yet may decide not to go to the polls if they believe that their candidate has already won. Or, if voters believe that their candidate has lost, they may think it's too late to make a difference. But elections can be very close, and every vote counts!

AND THE WINNER IS ...

The clock ticks as candidates wait anxiously at their festively decorated campaign headquarters for the election results to come in. When the winner is announced, the winning side roars with celebration. Music, balloons, streamers, and confetti fill the air.

Things are much quieter on the losing side. When a presidential election is over, the losing candidate concedes the election. This means that he or she accepts the loss. The losing candidate calls the winner and offers congratulations. The losing candidate then gives a speech to the public called a concession speech.

The winner of the election gives a very different kind of speech—a victory speech. He or she thanks everyone for their help with the campaign and talks about the changes that will happen when he or she takes office.

PLEASE BE PATIENT!

In 1960, the election results of John F. Kennedy over Richard M. Nixon weren't official until the afternoon of the next day. In the 2000 race between George W. Bush and Al Gore, the results weren't official until the 26th of November— almost 3 weeks later!

I WON!

Write your own victory speech. Include things such as new laws you hope to pass and changes you hope to see in the future.

I LOST!

Write your own concession speech. Include congratulations to the new president, and your ideas about what you will do in the future.

BECOMING PRESIDENT:
NOW WHAT HAPPENS?

Although the election takes place in November, the new president doesn't take office until January. From November until January, the new president is called the president-elect, and the current president is still in power. In January, the president-elect is inaugurated. An inauguration is the ceremony that marks the time that the president-elect officially becomes the president. The inauguration is held at the U.S. Capitol in Washington, D.C., and thousands of people attend.

The new president raises his or her right hand, places his or her left hand on the Bible, and takes the following oath of office:

"I do solemnly swear [or affirm] that I will faithfully execute the office of president of the United States, and will, to the best of my ability, preserve, protect, and defend the Constitution of the United States."

The president has worked long and hard to become president. The election is over and the time has come to do the job. But what exactly does the president do?

Here are some of the things the president does:

- **Meets with the leaders of other nations to write treaties and make agreements. (But the Senate needs to approve them.)**

- **Acts as chief of the government—the "boss" of all government workers.**

- **Serves as commander-in-chief of the U.S. military. (He can declare war but needs Congress to approve it.)**

- **Suggests new laws and encourages Congress to make them happen. (Congress has to approve these, too.)**

- **Approves or vetoes laws made by Congress. He can say, "Yes! That's a great idea!" or, "No way. I veto it."**

- **Chooses people to serve as U.S. ambassadors to other countries.**

- **Appoints people to run sections of government. This includes the Supreme Court justices. (The Senate has to agree on these, too.)**

E ven if you're too young to vote, you can still get involved with politics. In fact, you can probably get involved right in your own school.

❋ *Run for student council.* Most schools have student councils. They usually have a president, a vice president, a secretary, and a treasurer, all elected by their fellow students. Running for student council gives you a chance to learn to organize a campaign and even to speak in public! Not to mention that by being on a student council you can work to make your school a better place.

❋ *Join school groups.* For example, you could start or join a discussion group that focuses on world hunger. Or, you might participate in a debate about school policies, or about how to rate movies and videos. You could write opinion pieces for your school newspaper. You might find that one of these issues interests you so much, it leads you to a volunteer job or even a future career.

❋ *Volunteer for a political campaign.* There are plenty of things you can do for a campaign—help with mailings, make telephone calls, run errands,

Believe it or not, most people who are eligible to vote don't. The highest percentage of Americans ever to vote in a presidential election was only 37.8 percent. That was in 1964. **YOU** can change that. Encourage the adults in your life to vote. And when you turn 18, be a voter!

and more. You could also join a group that your favorite candidate supports, such as a local environmental group.

❋ *Contact a government leader.* Even though you are not old enough to vote for them, government officials have the responsibility to represent people of all ages who live in their district. If you feel strongly about an issue, contact the appropriate government official to let them know how you feel.

So now you know all about the election process, right? Well, you probably know a lot more than you did before. Now you can look at political advertising with a wise eye. You can understand why people are waving signs and shouting at their political conventions. You know how and when to vote. And just think, when you are old enough to vote in a political election, you'll have these tools to help you make a decision. And one thing you know for sure—voting is a very important way to have a say.

FOR MORE INFORMATION

Web Sites

Ben's Guide to U.S. Government for Kids
http://bensguide.gpo.gov/

FirstGov for Kids
www.kids.gov

Kids Voting U.S.A
www.kidsvotingusa.org

Take Your Kids to Vote
www.takeyourkidstovote.org

The White House
www.whitehouse.gov/kids/

Books

Giesecke, Ernestine. *National Government*. Heinemann Library, 2000.

Granfield, Linda. *America Votes: How Our President Is Elected*. Kids Can Press, 2003.

Henry, Christopher. *The Electoral College*. Franklin Watts, 1996.

Henry, Christopher. *Presidential Elections*. Franklin Watts, 1996.

Kielburger, Marc and Craig. *Take Action! A Guide to Active Citizenship*. John Wiley and Sons, 2002.

Maestro, Betsy. *The Voice of the People: American Democracy in Action*. Lohrop, Lee, and Shepard Books, 1996.

Pascoe, Elaine. *The Right to Vote*. Millbrook Press, 1997.

St. George, Judith. *So You Want to be President?* Philomel Books, 2000.

GLOSSARY

Ballot A form—paper or electronic—that voters use to cast their votes.

Candidate A person running for political office, such as president of the United States (or president of the student council!)

Campaign The organized effort to get a candidate elected.

Convention A meeting of the delegates of a political party to select their candidate.

Debate A public meeting in which candidates discuss and argue their viewpoints.

Delegate Representative of a political party who attends the national convention and selects the party's nominee for president.

Democracy A system of government in which power is shared by all of its citizens.

Democrat A member of the Democratic Party. The Democratic Party is one of two main political parties in the United States.

Electoral college The group of people, called electors, who directly vote for president of the United States. Their votes are guided by the way the people of their states have voted.

General election The main election—the one in which the winning candidate for president is decided.

Inauguration The formal ceremony that marks the beginning of a winning candidate's term as president.

Nominee The person that a party chooses to be its candidate in the general election. The nominees are chosen in the primary election.

Platform The principles and ideas that a candidate and his or her party feels are most important.

Political party An organized group of people with similar political viewpoints who work together to promote their ideas and to elect candidates who share their beliefs.

President-elect A candidate who has won the presidential election but who has not yet taken office.

Primary election The election in which voters of each political party choose the candidate from their party to run in the general (main) election.

Representative democracy A system in which voters elect people (such as president or members of Congress) to represent their views in government.

Republican A member of the Republican Party. The Republican Party is one of two main political parties in the United States.

Suffrage The right to vote. The Women's Suffrage Movement worked to gain this right for women.

Third party Any political party other than the Democratic Party or the Republican Party.

INDEX